The Science of Liquids & Solids

LIVING SCIENCE

Krista McLuskey

Weigl Publishers Inc.

Published by Weigl Publishers Inc.
123 South Broad Street, Box 227
Mankato, MN 56002
USA

Library of Congress Cataloging-in-Publication Data available upon request from the publisher.
Fax (507) 388-2746 for the attention of the Publishing Records Department.

ISBN 1-930954-11-5

Project Co-ordinator: Jared Keen
Series Editor: Celeste Peters
Copy Editor: Heather Kissock
Design: Warren Clark
Cover Design: Terry Paulhus
Layout: Lucinda Cage

Photograph Credits:
Corbis Images: page 16; Corel Corporation: cover (center), pages 4, 5 left, 6 left, 6 center left, 7, 8 top right, 9, 10 bottom, 12 top left, 14 top left, 14 bottom left, 14 bottom right, 15 bottom left, 18, 19, 22, 25 bottom left, 27 center right, 27 bottom; Digital Vision: pages 12 bottom, 13 left; Eyewire: cover (background), pages 26, 27 center left, 31; PhotoDisc: pages 5 right, 10 center left, 15 center right, 20, 23 left; Monique de St. Croix: pages 6 center right, 6 right, 8 bottom left, 8 bottom right, 21, 23 right, 24, 25 right, 28, 29, 30; Visuals Unlimited: pages 11 (Mark E. Gibson), 13 right (Mark S. Skalny), 14 top right (Richard C. Walters).

Printed in the United States of America

1 2 3 4 5 6 7 8 9 05 04 03 02 01

Contents

What Do You Know about Liquids and Solids?

Liquids are substances that flow. Water is the most common liquid on Earth. All living things must have water to stay alive. Oceans are homes for fish and plants. Lakes and rivers provide water to drink. Rainfall supplies some of the moisture crops need to grow.

A liquid has no shape of its own. It takes the shape of the solid that surrounds it.

Liquid lakes and solid mountains help form our world.

Solids are substances that hold their shape. The ground under our feet is a solid. The mountains on the **horizon** are solids. Our houses are solids, and so are many of the foods we eat.

Liquids and solids make up our world, and they often **interact**. Solid boats float on liquid streams. Solid sugar **dissolves** when it is stirred into a hot liquid, such as tea or coffee. An artist uses liquid paints on a solid canvas to create a masterpiece.

Solid bridges are built across liquid rivers. Bridges help people travel easily across water.

Liquids flow freely unless they are held in place by a solid.

Feeling Our World

People can feel the difference between liquids and solids by touching them. We touch many liquids and solids every day. Here are some examples of liquids and solids and words that might be used to describe them. Can you think of others?

Liquids

Tea	Milk Shake	Dish Soap	Pancake Syrup
• wet	• wet	• wet	• wet
• thin	• thick	• slippery	• sticky
• smooth	• smooth	• smooth	• smooth

Puzzler

Touching something tells us whether it is hard or soft, wet or dry, smooth or rough, and thick or thin. What else can touch tell us?

Answer:
Touch can tell us
if something is
hot or cold.

Solids

Kitten Fur	Carpet	Glass	Brick
• dry	• dry	• dry	• dry
• soft	• soft	• hard	• hard
• smooth	• rough	• smooth	• rough

Using Liquids and Solids

Almost everything we use in our daily lives is a liquid, a solid, or a combination of the two. People put liquids and solids to work in many ways.

Houses
are built of solid materials.
Wood, stone, dried clay or mud, ice, and palm leaves are some of the materials used

Inkjet Printers
use liquid ink to print an image from a computer screen.
The ink dries into a solid on paper, which is also a solid.

A Waterbed
has liquid water inside a solid plastic casing.
If the casing gets a hole in it, the water will flow out.

Candles
are solid objects that turn into a liquid as they burn.
They are usually made of wax, which is a solid substance that softens or **melts** when heated.

Activity

How Do You Use Liquids and Solids?
Think of five ways you used liquids today. Now think of five ways you used solids. Can you think of something you used that was not a liquid or a solid?

Cars, Buses, and Airplanes
use liquid fuel to make them move.
The fuel burns inside the machine's engine to create the energy that makes the machine go.

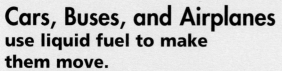

Swimming Pools
are solid forms that hold liquid water inside them.
Pools built into the ground are usually made of concrete. Pools built above the ground are usually made of plastics and metals.

Creative Careers

Artists turn liquids and solids into objects of beauty. Some artists work with a favorite liquid or solid, such as paint or wood. Others create art using both liquids and solids.

Painters use liquid paints to create pictures and designs on solid surfaces. As paint dries, it becomes a solid, too. At this point, the paint no longer flows and cannot be moved. The artist's work is ready for others to enjoy.

Painters use many liquid materials to create solid works of art.

A glassblower heats the solid ingredients of glass until they melt. These ingredients include sand and limestone. The liquid glass is blown and molded into creative shapes. As the liquid cools, it hardens into a solid again.

Ice sculptors carve designs into solid blocks of ice. This kind of art is not permanent. As soon as the Sun shines on it, the ice melts and becomes a liquid. Ice sculptors must save their art in photographs.

Glassblowers work with very hot materials. Glass melts at about 2200° Fahrenheit (1200° Celsius).

Activity

Do Your Own Research

Ask a parent or a teacher to help you find out more about these creative careers that make use of both liquids and solids:

- painter
- florist
- photographer
- sculptor
- chef

What Is the Matter?

Everything in the world is made of **matter**. Matter is anything that takes up space. Paper, orange juice, air, and mountains are all made of matter. Mud puddles and people are made of matter, too. How can mud puddles and people both be made of matter when they are so different from each other?

From crayons to galaxies, everything around us is made of matter.

Matter comes in different forms. Liquid and solid are two of the forms. Liquid and solid are possible **states of matter**.

People are made of both liquid matter and solid matter. Mud is, too.

Puzzler

There are actually three common states of matter. Can you name them?

Answer:
The most common states of matter are liquid, solid, and **gas**. The air we breathe is an example of a gas.

From One State to Another

Matter does not always stay in the same state. It can change from one state to another.

The heat of the Sun changes water in Earth's oceans, lakes, and rivers into a gas called water vapor. Water vapor rises into the sky and forms clouds. When water in the clouds cools, it falls back to Earth as liquid rain or solid snowflakes. Snow melts into liquid water. The water from rain and snow forms rivers and streams that flow back to the oceans.

Imagine that you are hiking on a warm summer day. You see a small stream winding through the forest. In winter, you bundle up and go for the same hike. You find that the stream has turned into ice. The stream was a liquid in summer but turned into a solid in winter. What caused the stream to change from one state of matter to another?

Heat is the key. Matter changes states by losing or gaining heat. When a liquid loses heat, it cools. If it cools enough, it **freezes** and becomes a solid. Liquid water freezes into solid ice when it cools.

When a solid gains heat, it warms up. If it warms up enough, a solid might melt and become a liquid. Solid ice melts into liquid water when it warms up.

Activity

Make Juice-sicles!
1. Pour orange juice into an ice cube tray.
2. Put a toothpick into each section of the tray.
3. Check your tray every half hour. How long does it take for the juice to freeze?

Icicles form when dripping water freezes.

Melted rock explodes out of a volcano as liquid lava. When lava reaches the air, it cools and becomes a solid again.

Go with the Flow

When spilled juice spreads across a table and drips onto the floor, it makes a big mess! Why do liquids flow, while solids keep their shape? All matter is made up of tiny particles called **molecules**. Molecules pack together in different ways to form liquids and solids.

Molecules are so small they can be seen only through an **electron microscope**.

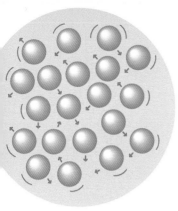

The molecules in liquids have room to slide around.

The molecules in liquids are not packed close together. Because their molecules have space to move around and slide past each other, liquids flow. Thin liquids, such as juice, flow faster than thick liquids, such as syrup. But all liquids flow.

The molecules in solids are packed close together. Because their molecules do not have any room to move around, solids keep their shape. If you knock over a glass of juice, the glass might roll across the table, but it will stay the same size and shape. Of course, the glass will change shape if it rolls off the table and hits the floor. It will break into smaller pieces of many different shapes!

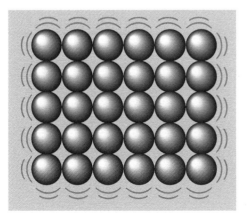

The tightly packed molecules in solids cannot move around.

Activity

How Fast Is the Flow?
What you will need:

- a funnel
- an empty milk jug
- one cup of water
- one cup of cooking oil
- one cup of syrup

1. Place the narrow end of the funnel into the milk jug.
2. Pour water through the funnel.
3. Watch how quickly the water flows into the milk jug.
4. Empty the milk jug.
5. Repeat steps 2 through 4 using cooking oil, then syrup, instead of water. Which liquids flow quickly? Which flow slowly? Can you guess why some liquids flow more quickly than others?

Shaping Our World

Liquids have no shape of their own. A liquid cannot be square, round, or glass-shaped by itself. It needs the help of a solid to have any shape at all. A river is shaped by the land around it. Juice is shaped by the carton or bottle that holds it. Liquids take on the shapes of the solids that surround them.

The syrup in a pitcher is shaped by the pitcher. Water in rivers is shaped by the surrounding solid ground.

Solids have shape. A chair is always chair-shaped unless someone breaks it. No matter what shape container you put a rock into, the rock keeps its own shape. The molecules in solids are packed so tightly they cannot move or flow. A solid object cannot change its shape.

A rock has its own shape. The shape of the rock stays the same unless the rock is crushed, broken, or worn away.

Puzzler

How can you change a solid into a liquid?

Answer:
Many solids can be changed into liquids by adding heat.

Liquid "Skin"

A liquid takes the shape of the solid surrounding it. So what gives a drop of water its shape? The molecules on the surface of the drop do. They are more attracted to the water inside the drop than they are to the air surrounding it. The surface molecules hold on tightly to other water molecules, creating **surface tension**. The outside of a drop of water acts like skin. This "skin" gives the drop of water its shape. Bubbles are also held together by surface tension.

Surface tension helps drops of water and bubbles hold their shape.

Surface tension does more than shape drops of liquid and bubbles. It also allows small insects to skate across the tops of ponds. The "skin" on a pond's surface is strong enough to support the weight of some insects. It bends around the feet of the insects, but it does not break.

This water strider can walk on water. Surface tension supports the insect's weight.

Moving On Up

Rain falls from clouds. Rivers run from high mountains to low oceans. A force called **gravity** pulls water downward. Does water ever flow against the pull of gravity? Does it ever flow from low places to higher places?

Yes! Water can flow upward. Plants need water from the ground to grow. They have little hollow tubes in their stems that draw water up through the roots and stems to the leaves.

Water moves upward through the stems of plants.

The molecules of water rise in the tubes because they are attracted more to the tube than to other water molecules. This attraction is called **capillary action**. The pull of capillary action on water is stronger than the pull of gravity. It allows the plant to absorb, or soak up, the water.

Capillary action in clothing fabrics pulls liquid **perspiration** away from the skin.

Activity

Pick a Color
1. Fill a vase almost to the top with water.
2. Add several drops of blue or red food coloring to the water.
3. Cut a little bit off the bottom of the stem of a white carnation.
4. Put the stem of the carnation into the colored water for four hours.

What color is the carnation after four hours? How and why do you think the color of the flower changed?

Tiny holes in a paper towel or a sponge absorb liquid by capillary action.

23

Mixing Liquids and Solids

Stir cocoa and sugar into warm milk. What happens? The liquid milk becomes brown and sweet. The solid cocoa powder and sugar disappear. Where do these solids go? They dissolve and become part of the liquid! The milk molecules move into the spaces between the cocoa and sugar molecules, making the solids break apart. The cocoa and sugar molecules spread evenly through the milk — and you have hot chocolate.

Many drinks are made by adding a small amount of a solid to a large amount of a liquid.

Water can dissolve more kinds of solids than any other liquid. Just look at Earth's oceans. The water is very salty. The salts dissolved in ocean water come from all over the world. They were once part of rocks and soils.

Not all solids, however, dissolve in water. Many solids keep their shape and do not dissolve in liquids at all. A plastic cup, for example, will not dissolve in or mix together with almost any liquid no matter how long the liquid sits in it.

Some solids hold their shape when liquids are added to them.

Certain solids can be removed from liquids. Salt, for example, can be taken out of oceans. Letting the liquid water **evaporate** leaves the solid salt behind.

Activity

Does It Dissolve?

Find ten small solids, such as salt grains, sugar crystals, pebbles, and rice. One at a time, stir each solid into a glass of warm water. Make a chart with the headings "Dissolves" and "Does Not Dissolve." List each solid you test under the correct heading.

Sink or Swim?

Heavy steel ships float across oceans. Yet a coin tossed into a wishing well sinks to the bottom. Why do some solids float, while others sink?

Cork, wood, and wax are some of the solids that float. They are lighter than an amount of water the same size they are. In other words, they are not as **dense** as water. Rocks, coins, and glass almost always sink in water. They are heavier than an amount of water the same size they are. These solids are more dense than water.

Because logs are less dense than water, they float.

Big ships are often made of steel, which is a dense material that sinks in water. How, then, do ships stay afloat? The bottom of a ship is very large and holds a lot of air inside. The combined weight of the steel and the air is less than an amount of water the same size. In other words, the ship is less dense than water — so it floats!

Fish have a little bag of air inside their bodies that keeps them from sinking or floating.

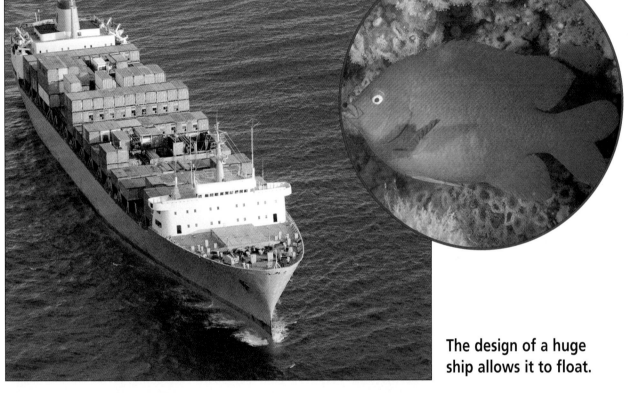

The design of a huge ship allows it to float.

Puzzler

Why do icebergs float?

Answer:
Water expands when it freezes. As water turns to ice, the water molecules move further apart. Ice, then, is less dense than water. So, like an ice cube in a glass of water, an iceberg floats.

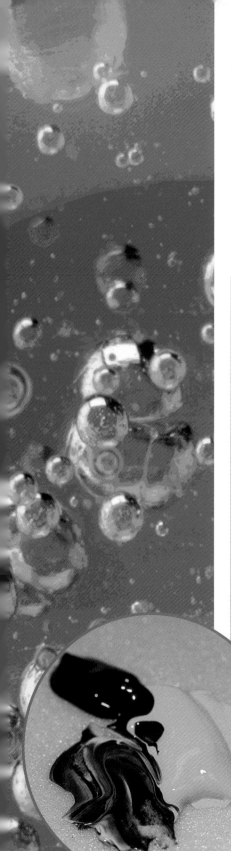

Mixed Up Liquids

Can liquids be mixed together? Sometimes they can. When two liquids such as cream and coffee are mixed together, they cannot be separated. These liquids mix together so well they form a new liquid.

Like cream and coffee, two colors of paint mixed together cannot be separated again.

Other liquids cannot be mixed together at all. When these liquids are combined, they form layers. The denser liquid sinks to the bottom. The less dense liquid floats to the top. Oil and vinegar, for example, form layers in a bottle of salad dressing, and grease floats like an island on top of dishwater.

Activity

Floating Liquids
1. Pour half a cup of water into a large, clear jar.
2. Add half a cup of vegetable oil.
3. Now add half a cup of maple syrup.
4. Watch the liquids separate.

Which liquid is the most dense? Which is the least dense? Which is in the middle?

When added to olive oil, balsamic vinegar floats on the surface of the oil.

A lava lamp contains liquids of different densities. When heated by the lamp's lightbulb, the lighter liquid forms bubbles that float to the top of the lamp.

Play It Safe!

Playing with liquids and solids can sometimes be dangerous. It is fun to swim, boat, ice skate, or ice fish on lakes or rivers, but people must be careful around water and ice. Water often has strong **currents** that can drag and hold a swimmer below the surface. Thin ice can crack open, plunging a person who is skating or fishing into freezing water. Rocks and logs underwater can tear the bottom of a boat, causing the boat to fill with water and sink.

Lifeguards help keep swimmers safe from some of the dangers of liquids and solids.

Whenever you play around water and ice, follow these important safety rules:

1. Never play alone around water or on ice. Make sure an adult is nearby.
2. Do not go into water that is too deep for your swimming skills.
3. Do not dive into water until you know it is deep enough. Ask an adult.
4. Look for posted signs that warn you to stay off ice. Also, look for signs of danger on the ice itself. For example, is there any water on top of the ice? Do you see any cracks in the ice? If you are not sure, do not step onto the ice.
5. If you fall through the ice, move to the edge of the hole. Spread your arms out over the ice and kick your legs until your body is up on the ice. Then crawl along the ice, keeping your weight spread out.
6. If someone else falls through the ice, never go onto the ice and try to help the person by yourself. Find an adult immediately.

Liquids and solids can be dangerous. Know how to protect yourself.

Glossary

capillary action: the upward flow of a liquid against the downward force of gravity.

currents: powerful flows of water moving in a particular direction.

dense: made up of parts packed very close together.

dissolves: becomes part of a liquid.

electron microscope: a device through which molecules can be seen with the human eye.

evaporate: change into a gas or vapor.

freezes: changes from a liquid to a solid by losing heat.

gas: a state, or form, of matter that is less dense than a liquid.

gravity: a force of nature that pulls all matter toward the center of Earth.

horizon: a line in the distance where Earth and sky seem to meet.

interact: do something with or for each other.

matter: what all substances are made of; anything that takes up space.

melts: changes from a solid to a liquid by gaining heat.

molecules: the smallest pieces of any substance that still behave like that substance.

perspiration: sweat.

states of matter: the different forms in which matter is found in nature.

surface tension: the attraction of molecules to each other on the surface of a liquid.

Index

Web Sites

ga.water.usgs.gov/edu/mwater.html

www.chem4kids.com/matter/state.html

www.mathmol.com/textbook/3gradecover.html

www.unmuseum.org/exboyant.htm

Some web sites stay current longer than others. For further web sites, use your search engines to locate the following topics: *density, glass, ice, liquids, matter, molecules, solids,* and *water.*